The Blues Singer

Some of America's Greatest Blues Songs
Complete Piano/Vocal Arrangements

Catalog #07-1083

ISBN# 1-56922-023-9

Printed in the United States of America

Produced by John L. Haag

Exclusive Distributor:
CREATIVE CONCEPTS PUBLISHING CORPORATION
6020-B Nicolle Street, Ventura, California 93003
Check out our Web site at *http://www.creativeconcepts.com* or you can Email us at *mail@creativeconcepts.com*

The Blues Singer

Contents

The Blues Singer

Contents

Ain't No Sunshine

Words and Music by Bill Withers

5

After You've Gone

Words and Music by Henry Creamer and Turner Layton

Baby, Get Lost

Words and Music by Leonard Feather

Baby, Won't You Please Come Home?

Words and Music by Charles Warfield and Clarence Williams

Bad Influence

Words and Music by Robert Cray and Mike Vannice

Beale Street Blues

Words and Music by W. C. Handy

(The) Birth of the Blues

Words by B.G. DeSylva and Lew Brown
Music by Ray Henderson

were search-ing for a diff-'rent tune, one that they could croon as on-ly they

can. _____ They on-ly had the rhy-thm so _____

rit.   *a tempo*

they start-ed sway-ing to and fro. _____

They did-n't know just what to use, that is how the blues re-al-ly be-

HERE'S THAT RAINY DAY

Deidre Cerul

Words by JOHNNY BURKE
Music by JAMES VAN HEUSEN

Toughest Girl Alive - Candye Kane

Southern Comfort - E.G. Knight

Biggest Part of Me - Anderson .No!

Come On Home - Billy Hector

Drowning All Star Joint - KB

I Want to (Do Everything for You) - Rosanne Pottie

Fuck, You're Dead - Howo Jordan

When Love Comes to Town

Ruby: Fleeing Roomful & Michele Parish

Don't get around much anymore: Duke Ellington

Straighten Up & Fly Right

My Old Flame

Do You Know What It Means to Miss New Orleans?

Words by Eddie DeLange
Music by Louis Alter

I nev-er had this kind-a feel-in', _____

With drag-gin' heart and brain a-reel-in'. _____ What's the mat-ter,

Call It Stormy Monday (Stormy Monday Blues)

Words and Music by Aaron T-Bone Walker

35

EXTRA LYRICS

2

Yes, the eagle flies on Friday,
And Saturday I go out to play __
Eagle flies on Friday,
And Saturday I go out to play..
Sunday I go to church,
Then I kneel down to pray.

3

Lord have mercy,
Lord have mercy on me __
Lord have mercy,
My heart's in misery.
Crazy 'bout my baby,
Yes, send her back to me.

Crazy Blues

Words and Music by Perry Bradford

Downhearted Blues

Words and Music by Lovie Austin and Alberta Hunter

Gee, but it's hard to love some-one when that some-one don't love you.

If I could on—ly find the man oh how hap-py I would be.

I'm so dis-gust-ed, heart-bro-ken, too.

To the Good Lord ev—'ry night I pray.

42

Additional Choruses (Ad lib.)

Chorus 3: Say, I ain't never loved but three {men / women} in my life.
No, I ain't never loved but three {men / women} in my life,
'Twas my {father, brother / mother, sister} and the {man / woman} who wrecked my life.

Chorus 4: 'Cause {he / she} mistreated me and {he / she} drove me from {he / she} door,
Ye, {he / she} mistreated me and {he / she} drove me from {he / she} door,
But the Good Book says you'll reap just what you sow.

Chorus 5: Oh, it may be a week and it may be a month or two,
Yes, it may be a week and it may be a month or two,
But the day you quit me honey, it's coming home to you.

Chorus 6: Oh, I walked the floor and I wrung my hands and cried,
Yes, I walked the floor and I wrung my hands and cried,
Had the down hearted blues and couldn't be satisfied.

I'm a Fool to Want You

Words and Music by Jack Wolf, Joel Herron and Frank Sinatra

Evil (Is Going On)

Words and Music by Willie Dixon

Farewell Blues

Words and Music by Elmer Schoebel, Paul Mares and Leon Roppolo

A Good Man is Hard to Find

Words and Music by Eddie Green

Got My Mojo Working

Words and Music by Preston Foster

I Ain't Got Nobody

Words by Roger Graham
Music by Spencer Williams and Dave Peyton

I'll sing sweet love songs, hon-ey, all the time, If you'll

come and be my sweet ba-by mine; 'Cause I

AIN'T GOT NO-BOD-Y, And no-bod-y

cares for me. Now me.

I Cried For You

Words and Music by Arthur Freed, Gus Arnheim and Abe Lyman

I Got It Bad (And That Ain't Good)

Words and Music by Duke Ellington and Paul Francis Webster

I'm Your Hoochie Coochie Man

Words and Music by Willie Dixon

gon - na make 'em jump and shout.
lead me by the hand.
that you're gon - na see.

Then the world could know____
Then the world will know____
I've got sev-en hun-dred dol-lars, ba-by,____

F7   B♭7

what this was all a-bout.__
I'm the hoo-chie coo-che man.__ } Lord,__ I'm here,__ oh yeah,__ Ev-'ry-bod-y knows__ I'm
don't you __ mess with me.__ }

F   C7   B♭7

here,__ oh Lord,_____ 'Cause I'm a hoo-chie coo-che man,__ Ev-'ry-bod-y knows__ I'm

1, 2. F   Cm7   F   Cm7   3. F   Cm7   F7

here.__   here._____

rall.

I Never Loved a Man (the Way I Love You)

Words and Music by Ronnie Shannon

It's Just a Matter of Time

Words and Music by Clyde Otis, Brook Benton and Belford Hendricks

The Jazz-Me Blues

Words and Music by Tom Delaney

I Wonder Where My Easy Rider's Gone

Words and Music by Shelton Brooks

Memphis Blues

Words and Music by W. C. Handy

You want to be my man (gal) you got to give me for-ty dol-lars down. You want to be my man, (gal), you'll give me for-ty dol-lars down. If you don't

We don't care _ what Mis - ter Crump don't 'low _

we gon - na bar'l - house an - y how, _ Mis - ter

Crump don't 'low _ no
Crump can go _ and

eas - y rid - ers here.
catch him - self _ some

air.

Key to the Highway

Words and Music by Big Bill Broonzy and Chas. Segar

2. I'm goin' back to the border
   Where I'm better known.
   Though you haven't done nothin',
   Drove a good man away from home.

3. Oh, gimme one more kiss, mama,
   Just before I go,
   'Cause when I leave this time,
   I won't be back no more.

4. (Repeat Verse 1)

Lovesick Blues

Words and Music by Irving Mills and Cliff Friend

Fast Country ♩ = 132

I got a feel-ing called the blues, _____ oh, _____ Lord, _____ since my ba-by said good - bye. And Lord, I don't know what I'll do. _____ All I do is sit and cry, _____ oh _____ Lord. _____

Mercy, Mercy, Mercy

Words by Gail Fisher Levy and Vincent Levy
Music by Josef Zawinul

Misty Blue

Words and Music by Bob Montgomery

Mercy on Me

Words and Music by Champion Jack Dupree

Lord I ask ____ you for one fa - vor ____ Lord for

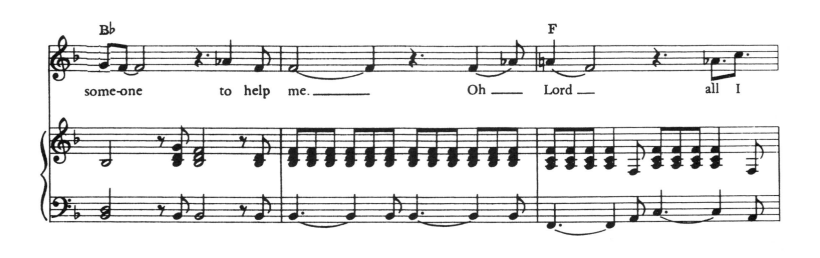

some-one to help me. _____ Oh ____ Lord ____ all I

need _____ in this world is a help-ing hand.

Oh Lord all of my

life ___ I been in trou - ble ___ as they go

by I been mis - treat - ed ___ Oh ___

Lord___ treat-ed like a dog. So bye and

bye when my day is come yeah! And I leave,___ leave this world be-

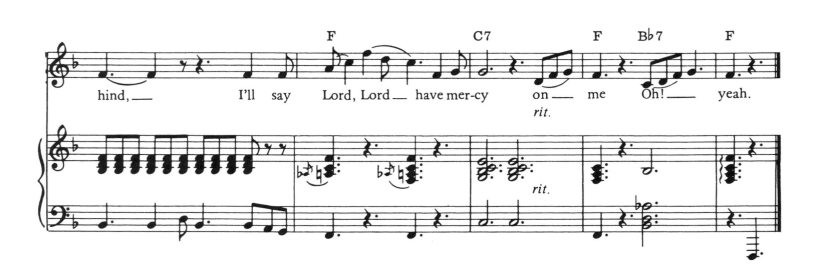

hind,___ I'll say Lord, Lord___ have mer-cy on___ me Oh!___ yeah.

Midnight Special

Arranged and Adapted by Johnny Weber

2. Well if you're ever in Houston,
   You'd better walk on by
   Oh, you'd better not gamble, boy
   I say you'd better not fight.
   Well now, the sheriff, he'll grab you
   And his boys will pull you down
   And then before you know it
   You're penitentiary-bound.
      (To Chorus) A-let the Midnight Special etc.

3. Here comes Miss Lucy
   How in the world do you know?
   I know by her apron
   And by the dress she wore.
   An umbrella on her shoulder
   A piece of paper in her hand
   She gonna see the sheriff
   To try to free her man.
      (To Chorus) A-let the Midnight Special etc.

My Babe

Words and Music by Willie Dixon

Night Life

Words and Music by Willie Nelson, P. Buskirk and W. Breeland

Nobody

Words by Alex Rogers
Music by Bert A. Williams

Nobody Knows You When You're Down and Out

Words and Music by Jimmie Cox

Once I lived the life of a mil - lion - aire,__

Spend-ing my mon-ey and I did-n't care.__ Tak - ing my friends out for a

118

Rollin' and Tumblin'

Words and Music by McKinley Morganfield (Muddy Waters)

St. James Infirmary

Words and Music by Sonny Potter

127

St. Louis Blues

Words and Music by W. C. Handy
New Popular Arrangement by Leonard Moss

pow - der and all her store ___ bought hair, ___

that man ___ that I love would -n't have gone no - where.

Chorus

Got the Saint Lou - is Blues just as

blue as I ___ can be. ___ That

old Ken -tuck -y Col' -nel loves his rocks loves his rocks and rye, And I

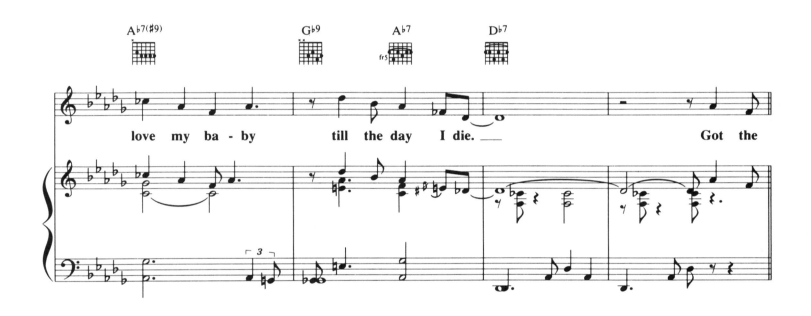

love my ba - by till the day I die. ___ Got the

Saint Lou -is Blues ___ *(in the morn -ing)* Saint Lou -is Blues ___ *(in the eve -ning)*

134

ADDITIONAL CHORUS LYRICS

Oh, ashes to ashes and dust to dust,
I said ashes to ashes and dust to dust.
If my blues don't get you, my jazzing must.

See See Rider (C.C. Rider)

Arranged and Adapted by Sonny Potter

The Seventh Son

Words and Music by Willie Dixon

Moderately, with a beat

Now, ev-'ry-bod-y's talk-in' 'bout the sev-enth son, In the whole round world there is on-ly one. I'm the one, yes, I'm the one, _____ I'm the one, I'm the one, The

Since You've Been Gone

Words and Music by Aretha Franklin and Ted White

144

Shorty George

Words and Music by Sam Hoskins

Well - a, Short - y George, ___ he ain't no friend of mine, ___ Well - a, Short - y George, ___ he ain't no friend of mine, ___

Shorty George, he done been here and gone,
Yes, Shorty George, he done been here and gone,
Lord, he left many a poor man a great long way from home.

My mama died when I was a lad,
My mama died when I was a lad,
And ever since I been to the bad.

Well, my babe caught the Katy, I caught the Santa Fe(e),
Well, she caught the Katy and I caught the Santa Fe(e),
Well, you can't quit me, baby, can't you see?

Well, I went to Galveston—work on the Mallory Line,
Went to Galveston—Lord, on the Mallory Line,
Babe, you can't quit me—ain't no use tryin'.

Shorty George, travelin' through the land,
Shorty George, he's travelin' through the land,
Alway's lookin' to pick some poor woman's man.

When I get back to Dallas, I'm gonna walk and tell,
When I get back to Dallas, gonna walk and tell,
That the Fort Bend bottom is a burning hell.

Some of These Days

Words and Music by Shelton Brooks

Spoonful

Words and Music by Willie Dixon

Medium beat

1. It could be a spoon – ful of dia – monds,
   could be a spoon – ful of cof – fee,
   could be a spoon – ful of wa – ter,

Could be a spoon – ful of gold.
Could be a spoon – ful of tea.
Saved from the des – ert sand.

Just a lit – tle spoon of your
Just a lit – tle spoon of your
But one spoon of them

pre – cious love___ sat – is – fies___ my soul.
pre – cious love___ is good e – nough___ for me.
for – ty fives___ saved you from an – oth – er man.

Men

Stormy Weather

Words by Ted Koehler
Music by Harold Arlen

Slow Lament

Don't know why there's no sun up in the sky, Storm-y Weath-er,

Since my {man gal} and I ain't to-geth-er, keeps rain-in' all the time.

Life is bare, gloom and mis-'ry ev-'ry-where, Storm-y Weath-er,

155

Sugar Blues

Words by Lucy Fletcher
Music by Clarence Williams

'Tain't Nobody's Biz-ness, If I Do

Words and Music by Porter Grainger and Everett Robbins

Teacher's Blues

Arranged and Adapted by Johnny Weber

Teach - er, Teach - er, why are you so poor? — Teach - er, Teach-er, why are you so poor? —

When it comes to un - ions _____ you're an am - a - teur.

Now,

Now, Mister Teacher, why don't you organize?
Say, Teacher, Teacher, why don't you organize?
Don't sit around and watch those prices rise.

Now, unions are for workers, but a teacher has prestige;
Yes, unions are for workers, but a teacher has prestige;
He can feed his kids on that old *noblesse oblige.*

So he wears a white collar, he's treated with respect;
He wears a white collar, he's treated with respect;
Financially—he's solid wrecked.

A teacher's collar is white, but Lord, it sure is frayed;
A teacher's collar is white, but Lord, it sure is frayed;
Now, could it be the pittance he is paid?

Well, Teacher, Teacher, be a happy drudge;
Come on now, Teacher, be a happy drudge;
Stuff yourself with that intellectual sludge.

Here's the source of our society's high-minded low-paid knowledge,
That's where it comes from, that high-minded low-paid knowledge,
That underprivileged character, the guy who teaches college.

Got those teacher's blues, those blues are on my mind,
Yes, those teacher's blues, those blues are on my mind,
Inflation's here, and left me far behind.

There'll Be Some Changes Made

Words by Billy Higgins
Music by W. Benton Overstreet

They say don't change the old
They say the old-time things

for the new, ___
are the best, ___

But I've found out that this will,
That may be ver-y good for

nev-er do ___
all the rest ___

When you grow old you don't last long ___
But I'm goin' let the old things be ___

Think

Words and Music by Aretha Franklin and Ted White

A Worried Man

Arranged and Adapted by Johnny Weber

It takes a wor - ried man to sing a wor - ried

song, It takes a wor - ried man to sing a wor - ried song, It

takes a wor - ried man to sing a wor - ried song, I'm wor - ried now

but I won't be wor - ried long.

Trouble, No More

Words and Music by McKinley Morganfield (Muddy Waters)

Moderately Bright (but in four)

175

Wabash Blues

Words by Dave Ringle
Music by Fred Meinken

Yellow Dog Blues

Words and Music by W.C. Handy

E'er since Miss Su - san John-son lost her Jock-ey, Lee, _ there has been

I know the Yel-low Dog Dis - trict like a book, _ in - deed I

Work Song

Words by Oscar Brown, Jr.
Music by Nat Adderley

With a heavy beat

Verse:

1. Break-in' up big rocks___ on uh chain gang,   Break-in' rocks an'
2. I com-mit the crime,___ Lawd o' need-in',   Crime o' be-in'
3. Judge he say, "Five years___ hard___ la-bor,   On the chain gang
4. Wan-na' see my sweet___ hon-ey ba-by,   Wan-na' break this

serv-in' my time.   Break-in' rocks ou' chere___ on the chain gang,
hun-gry and poor.   Left the gro-cer store-man a' bleed-in'
you goin' t' go."   Heard the judge say, "Five___ years o' la-bor."
chain off an' run.   Wan-na' lay down some-where it's sha-dy,

'Cause I been con- vict - ed o' crime.
When he caught me rob - bin' his store.
Heard my wom- an scream, ___ "Law - dy, no!"
Lawd, it sure is hot ___ in the sun.

Chorus:

Hol' it stead-y right there ___ while I hit it. There! I reck-on that ___

ought-a git it. Been work-in' ___ an' work-in', But I still ___

___ got so terr-'ble long to go. ___

The Wang-Wang Blues

Words and Music by Gus Mueller, Buster Johnson and Henry Busse

Worried Life Blues

Words and Music by Maceo Merriweather